حائية ابن أبي داود

The Ḥā'iyya of ibn Abī Dāwūd

This edition features the original Arabic poem, accompanied by a versified English translation and a brief explanation. Additionally, it includes the translator's chain of narration back to the original author.

حائية ابن أبي داود

The Ḥā'iyya of ibn Abī Dāwūd

Translation and explanation: Joe W. Bradford

Last Updated: 30 June 2024

ISBN-13: 979-8-9898696-2-6

Published by: Origem Publishing

Cover Image: In 1911, a photograph was taken of the Minaret of Sūq al-Ghazal (The Yarn Bazaar) in Baghdad. This minaret is considered the oldest in Baghdad and was originally part of the Caliph Mosque, constructed during the reign of Caliph al-Muktafī between 288 and 294 AH. Unfortunately, the mosque was destroyed in 656 AH by Hulagu during the sacking of the city. The present-day minaret was reconstructed by Abagha, Hulagu's son, between 663 and 680 AH. The photograph was taken by an unnamed German photographer and can be found in the public domain through Wikimedia.org. It was used on this cover to give the reader an approximation to what the author may likely have seen in his lifetime while teaching in the mosques of Baghdad.

Cover design: Salim Abul Salihat

Contents

Introduction 7

The Ḥā'iyya and its provenance 7

Manuscript of the Text 9

My work in this book 10

A Short Biography of Ibn Abī Dāwūd 11

My Isnād to the Author of this poem 13

The Arabic Text 15

The Beginning of the Annotated Text 18

Al-Ajurri's Attestation of the Text 18

Holding Fast to the Rope of Allah 19

Islam is Based on Submission 20

Allah's Speech is Uncreated 21

Saying "My recitation of the Quran is created." 23

Allah Will Be Seen by the Believers 24

Negating Semblance in Allah's Attributes 25

Evidence is Found in Authentic Reports 26

Allah's Right Hand is Not Diminished 28

Allah's Descends As Befits His Majesty 29

The Evidence for This From Ḥadīth 30

Allah's Forgiveness & Bounty 31

Adhering to the Understanding of the Salaf 32

The Status of the Four Caliphs 33

The Status of the Companions 35

The Ten Promised Paradise 36
Revering and Respecting the Companions 37
The Evidence for the Companions' Status 38
Belief in Qadr, a Pillar of Faith 39
Belief in the Last Day and All It Entails 40
Allah's Favor on the People of Tawḥīd 41
Those Who Enter Paradise Despite No Actions 42
The Prophet's Intercession for Mankind 43
Affirming the Punishment of the Grave 43
Not Excommunicating Believers Due to Sin 44
The Misguidance of the Khawārij 45
The Misguidance of the Murjia 46
Faith is Comprised of Beliefs and Actions 47
Faith Increases and Decreases 48
Avoiding Personal Opinion in Faith 49
Embodying High Character and Avoiding Flippancy 50
Taking This Creed to Heart 51
Ibn Abī Dāwūd's proclamation of his creed 52
Translator's Note 53

بسم الله الرحمن الرحيم

Introduction

All praise is due to Allah, the Lord of the worlds. The ultimate outcome belongs to the righteous. Blessings and peace be upon the leader of messengers, our Prophet Muhammad, and upon his family and all his companions.

The Ḥā'iyya and its provenance

This poem, known as "Al-Ḥā'iyya," is a poetic composition where each line ends in the letter Ḥ (ح). Authored by the accomplished scholar, the proficient preserver, and the sheikh of Baghdād, 'Abdullah ibn Abī Dāwūd Sulaymān ibn Al-Ash'ath, Al-Sijistāni (d. 316 AH), may Allah have mercy upon them both, it has been continuously transmitted from the time of the author until today.

This poem is widely recited and holds a prestigious position among scholars past and present. It has been consistently and concurrently transmitted from Ibn Abī Dāwūd through numerous knowledgeable scholars, at the forefront of them three of the author's own students: Abu Bakr Al-Ājurrī (d. 360 AH), Ibn Baṭṭa (d. 387 AH), and Ibn Shāhīn (d. 385 AH).

This poem is not only representative of the beliefs held by Ibn Abī Dāwūd, but those of his father Abu Dāwūd, Imam Aḥmad ibn Ḥanbal, and the scholars prior to them. It is a definitive work that represents not only what the beliefs of the Ḥanābila were, but what the beliefs of Ahl al-Ḥadīth and the scholars of the earliest generations of Islam were.

Al-Dhahabi (d. 748 AH), may Allah have mercy upon him, mentioned and highlighted the significance of this poem stating, "This poem is dependably narrated from its author by Al-Ājurrī, who also explained it. Abu Abdullah Ibn Baṭṭa also discussed it in 'Al-Ibānah,' who also wrote an explanation of it." Ibn Shāhīn also mentioned the poem in its entirety in his book Sharḥ Madhāhib Ahl al-Sunna.

Additionally, Imam Al-Saffārīnī (d. 1188 AH) wrote an explanation of it, published in two volumes under the title 'Lawā'iḥ Al-Anwār Al-Saniyya Wa Lawāqiḥ Al-Afkār Al-Suniyya." There are several other works on the poem as well that I will not mention here for brevity.

Manuscript of the Text

The following is a sample of the Al-Ḥā'iyya from Kitab al-Sharī'a by al-Ājurri, found in NurOsmania Library, (Nuruosin Section, Location No. 867/1-3, Old Registration No. 1196, Classification No. 297.2 = 927). As mentioned, al-Ājurri was a student of Ibn Abī Dawūd through whom my isnad to the text is transmitted:

My work in this book

I've presented Ibn Abī Dāwūd's poem here in its original Arabic, relying on Al-Ājurrī's text. Along with an attempt at translating it into versified English, I've followed that up with a brief explanation that clarifies the author's intent. I've added topical headers to each line of the poem in the table of contents, to make references to the poem's stanzas easier.

In this work I've relied on my notes from studying the book under Sh. AbdulRaḥman al-Barrāk at Masjid Shaikh al-Islam in Riyādh in the year 1423H/2002CE as well as the explanation of my teacher Sh. AbdulRazzāq al-Badr which he gifted to me after teaching it in Sharjah in 1424H/2003CE.

By translating and annotating this work I wanted to accomplish a few things. First, I wanted to answer the call of my student Abdullah ibn Mo'taz al-Hallak, who requested to study the book, someone most deserving to be answered. Second, I want to provide an accessible translation to students and teachers interested in it. Lastly, I want to highlight a short yet seminal text from one of the Salaf on the issues of belief, as all good is found in following their path.

Allah alone is whom I ask for acceptance and support.

وصلّى الله على نبينا محمد وعلى اله وصحبه وسلم.

Joe Bradford

A Short Biography of Ibn Abī Dāwūd

Abu Bakr ʻAbdullah ibn Sulaimān ibn al-Ashʻath al-Sijistāni, son of the famed Imam Abu Dāwūd, author of the Sunan. He was born in Sijistān in 230H, and accompanied his father as a child, traversing the east and west in pursuit of knowledge. He visited Asfahān, Baghdād, Kūfa, Makka, Madīna, Syria, Egypt, as well other places.

He settled in Baghdād, and the first scholar therein he learned from was Muḥammad ibn Aslam al-Ṭusi; making his father very happy. He had high ambitions as a young man and learned from some of the greatest scholars of his time. His teachers include his father, as well as Aḥmad ibn Ṣālih, Muḥammad ibn Bashār, Amr ibn ʻUthmān al-Ḥimṣi, Isḥāq al-Kawsaj, ʻAmr ibn Ali al-Fallās, and Muhammad ibn Yahya al-Dhuhali. His students include Ibn Ḥibbān (author of the Saḥīḥ), Abu al-Ḥasan al-Dāraquṭni, Ibn Baṭṭa, Ibn Shāhīn, Al-Ājurrī, and others.

He was a Ḥāfiẓ of ḥadīth, proficient in his memory and recollection. His student Ibn Shāhīn recounts that for two years Ibn Abī Dāwūd would dictate, from memory, ḥadīth to him never once seeing him carrying a book.

Abu Muhammad al-Khallāl said about him "Ibn Abī Dāwūd was the Imam of Iraq's people, someone the Sulṭān erected the Minbar for; despite there being people with more narrations that him, they did not compare to him in proficiency and skill." Al-Khatib al-Baghdadi said about him "He was a jurist, a scholar, and a Ḥāfiẓ." Al-Dhahabi said "He was from the oceans of knowledge, as some even preferred him to his father!" He also said, "He wrote many works; the leadership of the Ḥanābila in Iraq was entrusted to him," and "...the man was from the major scholars of the Muslims and from the most trustworthy of their Ḥuffāẓ."

His beliefs were clearly those of Ahl al-Ḥadīth, following in the footsteps of his father and the scholars before him. He says at the end of this poem:

> *This is my belief, and the belief of my father, and the belief of Aḥmad ibn Ḥanbal, and the belief of the scholars we've met, and that of the scholars we have not met but was transmitted to us from them; anyone claiming about me other than this has lied.*

His works include this poem, as well as al-Sunan, Kitāb al-Ba'th wa al-Nushūr, Kitāb al-Maṣāḥif, Shir'at al-Maqāri', and al-Nāsikh wal-Mansūkh.

He died in Baghdad in the month of Dhul-Ḥijja in the year 316H at seventy-eight years old, leaving behind three sons and five daughters. It was said that some three hundred thousand or more prayed over his Janāza.

My Isnād to the Author of this poem

I narrate this poem back to its author through two of my Mashāyikh:

1) From Sh. Ghāzi ibn AbdelGhani ibn AbdulSattār al-Dehlawi with Abdullah ibn Mo'taz reading to him while I listened, from Sh. AbdulHayy al-Kattāni with his Isnād to Abu Bakr al- Ājurri from Ibn Abi Dawud directly:

أنشدنا غازي بن عبد الغني بن عبد الستار الدهلوي بقراءة عبد الله بن معتز الحلاق عليه، عن الحافظ عبد الحي الكتاني، عن عبد الله بن إدريس السنوسي وأحمد بن عثمان أبي الخير العطار، كلاهما عن محدث الهند نذير حسين الدهلوي، عن محمد إسحاق الدهلوي ، عن عبد العزيز بن الشاه ولي الله الدهلوي، عن أبيه، عن أبي طاهر بن إبراهيم الكوراني، عن أبيه، عن سلطان المزاحي، عن أحمد بن خليل السبكي، عن النجم الغيطي، عن الزين زكريا الأنصاري، عن ابن الفرات، عن محمود بن خليفة المنبجي، عن الحافظ الدمياطي، عن الوجيه منصور بن سليم الهمداني، أنا أبو بكر محمد بن سعيد الخازن، إجازة من بغداد أخبرتنا شهدة، إجازة أنا أبو الحسين أحمد بن عبد القادر بن يوسف، عن الآجري، إجازة قال: أنشدنا أبو بكر بن أبي داود.

2) From Sh Sa'ad el-Din ibn Muhammad Kamāl Hassanin with me reading to him, from Sh. Abdullah ibn Sālih al-Obaid with his Asānid to Ibn Shāhīn from Ibn Abi Dawud.

أنشدنا الشيخ سعد الدين بن محمد كمال بن رزيقة حسنين بقراءتي عليه، قال اروي الحائية سماعا بقراءة غيري عن شيخنا د. عبد الله صالح العبيد وأخبره بها العلامة

الفقيه المعمر عبد الله بن عبد العزيز بن عقيل النجدي الحنبلي غير مرة بالرياض عن عبد الحق الهاشمي عن أحمد بن عبد الله بن سالم البغدادي عن الشيخ عبد الرحمن بن حسن بن الإمام محمد بن عبد الوهاب عن جده عن عبد الله بن إبراهيم الشمري عن أبي المواهب الحنبلي عن النجم الغزي عن والده بدر الدين الغَزِّي عن أبي الفتح المِزِّي عن عائشة بنت محمد ابن عبد الهادي المقدسية عن الحافظ محمد بن أحمد بن عثمان الذهبي قال أنشدنا أبو العباس أحمد بن عبد الحميد قال أنشدنا الإمام أبو محمد بن قدامة سنة ثمان عشرة وستمائة ، أخبرتنا فاطمة بنت علي الوِقَاياتِي أخبرنا علي بن بيان أخبرنا الحسين بن علي الطَنَاجِيْرِي حدثنا أبو حفص بن شاهين أنشدنا أبو بكر بن أبي داود لنفسه. ويرويها الشيخ العبيد بدرجة أعلى عن محمد بن عبد الرحمن بن إسحاق آل الشيخ النجدي الحنبلي بسنده قراءة عليه بالرياض. ويرويها كذلك عالية جدا بثلاث درجات عن المحدث المعمر أحمد بن نصر النعماني قراءة عليه بالمدينة المنورة بسنده.

With these chains I narrate the poem back to its author through two of his direct students, Ibn Shāhīn and Abu Bakr al-Ājurri, may Allah have mercy on them both, on our teachers, their teachers, and all those we narrate through back to Ibn Abi Dawud, Amīn.

The Arabic Text

قال أبو بكر الآجرّي في كتابه الشريعة:

قد كان أبو بكر بن أبي داود رحمه الله أنشدنا قصيدة قالها في السنة وهذا موضعها، وأنا أذكرها ليزداد بها أهل الحق بصيرة وقوة إن شاء الله : أملى علينا أبو بكر بن أبي داود في مسجد الرصافة في يوم الجمعة لخمس بقين من شعبان سنة تسع وثلاثمائة ، فقال تجاوز الله عنه:

1 تمسك بحبلِ الله واتبعِ الهُدى * ولا تكُ بدعياً لعلك تُفلحُ

2 ودِنْ بكتابِ الله والسننِ التي * أتت عنْ رسول الله تنجو وتربحُ

3 وقل غيرُ مخلوقٍ كلام مليكنا * بذلك دان الأتقياء وأفصحوا

4 ولا تكُ في القرآن بالوقف قائلاً * كما قال أتْباعٌ لجهمٍ وأسجحُوا

5 ولا تقل القرآن خلْقٌ قرأْتُهُ * فإن كلام اللهِ باللفظ يُوضحُ

6 وقل يتجلى الله للخلقِ جهرةً * كما البدر لا يخفى وربك أوضحُ

7 وليس بمولودٍ وليس بوالدٍ * وليس له شِبْهٌ تعالى المُسبحُ

8 وقد يُنكِر الجهمي هذا وعندنا * بمصداقِ ما قلنا حديثٌ مصرحُ

9 رواه جريرٌ عن مقالِ مُحمدٍ * فقُلْ مِثل ما قد قال في ذاك تنْجحُ

10 وقد ينكرُ الجهمي أيضاً يمينَهُ * وكِلتا يديه بالفواضلِ تنْفحُ

11 وقل ينزلُ الجبارُ في كلِّ ليلةٍ * بلا كيفَ جلَّ الواحدُ المُتمَدحُ

12 إلى طَبَقِ الدنيا يمُنُّ بفضلهِ * فتُفرجُ أبوابُ السماءِ وتُفتحُ

13 يقولُ أَلا مُستغفرٌ يَلقَ غافراً * ومُستمنحٌ خيراً ورِزْقاً فُيمنحُ

14 روى ذاك قومٌ لا يردُّ حديثُهم * ألا خابَ قومٌ كذبوهم وقُبِّحوا

15 وقل: إنَّ خير النَّاسِ بعد محمَّدٍ * وزيراهُ قِدَماً ثم عثمانُ الارجَحُ

16 ورابعهُمْ خيرُ البريَّة بعدهُم * عليٌّ حليفُ الخيرِ بالخيرِ مُنْجِحُ

17 وإنَّهم للرَّهطُ لا ريبَ فيهمُ * على نُجبِ الفردوسِ بالنُّور تسرحُ

18 سعيدٌ وسعدٌ وابن عوفٍ وطلحةٌ * وعامرُ فهرٍ والزبيرُ الممدَّح

19 وقل خير قولٍ في الصحابة كلِّهم * ولا تك طعَّاناً تعيبُ وتجرحُ

20 فقد نطقَ الوحيُ المُبينُ بفضلِهم * وفي الفتح آيٌّ للصَّحابةِ تمدحُ

21 وبالقدرِ المقدورِ أيقِن فإنَّه * دِعامةُ عِقدِ الدِّين والدِّينُ أفيحُ

22 ولا تُنكِرَنْ جهلاً نكيراً ومُنكَراً * ولا الحوْضَ والميزانَ إنك تُنصحُ

23 وقُلْ يُخرِجُ اللهُ الْعظيمُ بِفَضلِهِ * مِنَ النارِ أجْساداً مِنَ الفَحْمِ تُطرحُ

24 عَلى النهرِ في الفِرْدوسِ تَحْيَا بِمائِهِ * كَحِبِّ حَمِيلِ السَّيْلِ إِذْ جاءَ يَطْفَحُ

25 وإن رسولَ اللهِ للخَلْقِ شَافِعٌ * وقُلْ في عَذابِ القَبْرِ حَقّ مُوضحُ

26 ولاَ تُكْفِرنْ أَهلَ الصلاةِ وإِنْ عَصَوْا * فَكُلهُمُ يَعْصِي وذُو العَرشِ يَصفَحُ

27 ولَا تَعتقِدْ رأيَ الْخَوارجِ إِنهُ * مقَالٌ لِمَنْ يَهواهُ يُردي ويَفْضَحُ

28 ولا تكُ مُرْجيًّا لَعُوبا بدينهِ * ألاَ إِنما المُرْجِيُّ بِالدينِ يَمْزَحُ

29 وقلْ : إنما الإِيمانُ : قولٌ ونيةٌ * وفعلٌ عَلَى قولِ النبي مُصَرحُ

30 ويَنْقُصُ طوراً بالمَعَاصِي وتَارةً * بِطَاعَتِهِ يَنمي وفي الوَزْنِ يَرْجَحُ

31 ودعْ عَنْكَ آراءَ الرجالِ وقَوْلَهُمْ * فقولُ رسولِ اللهِ أزكَى وأَشْرحُ

32 ولا تَكُ مِن قوْمٍ تلهّوْا بدينِهِمْ * فَتَطْعَنَ في أهلِ الحَديثِ وتقدحُ

33 إِذَا مَا اعْتقدْت الدهْرَ يا صَاحِ هذهِ * فأَنْت عَلَى خَيْرٍ تبيتُ وتُصْبِحُ

ثم قال لنا أبو بكر بن أبي داود : هذا قولي وقول أبي وقول أحمد بن حنبل وقول من أدركنا من أهل العلم ومن لم ندرك ممن بلغنا عنه ، فمن قال علي غير هذا فقد كذب. ا.هـ.

The Beginning of the Annotated Text

Al-Ajurri's Attestation of the Text

قال أبو بكر الآجرّي في كتابه الشريعة:

قد كان أبو بكر بن أبي داود رحمه الله أنشدنا قصيدة قالها في السنة وهذا موضعها، وأنا أذكرها ليزداد بها أهل الحق بصيرة وقوة إن شاء الله : أملى علينا أبو بكر بن أبي داود في مسجد الرصافة في يوم الجمعة لخمس بقين من شعبان سنة تسع وثلاثمائة ،

فقال تجاوز الله عنه:

Abu Bakr al-Ājurri, in his book Kitāb al-Sharī'a, said:

Abu Bakr Ibn Abī Dāwūd – may Allah have mercy on him – rehearsed to us this ode he composed about the Sunna. I will mention it here so that the people of truth may increase in their conviction and strength, Allah willing. Abu Bakr ibn Abī Dāwūd dictated to us in the al-Raṣāfa masjid, on Friday with just five days left in Sha'bān in the year three hundred and nine.

He said, may Allah absolve him:

Holding Fast to the Rope of Allah

1- تمسك بحبلِ الله واتبعِ الهُدى ❋ ولا تكُ بدعياً لعلك تُفلحُ

Hold onto the rope of Allah, follow His guidance,

And do not be an innovator, perhaps you will succeed.

Grasping firmly to Allah's rope as Allah commanded in the Quran when he said "And grasp tight to the rope of Allah and do not split up..." as differing in faith and splitting into factions is an innovation. Success is found in following the Quran and Sunnah, and failure is found in innovation and the fanciful ideas that attempt to bypass the sources of revelation.

explanation

This is derived from the saying of Allah: "And hold firmly to the rope of Allah all together and do not become divided. And remember the favor of Allah upon you—when you were enemies and He brought your hearts together and you became, by His favor, brothers. And you were on the edge of a pit of the Fire, and He saved you from it. Thus does Allah make clear to you His verses that you may be guided" (Āl-ʻImrān: 103). And His saying: "But those who hold fast to the Book and establish prayer—indeed, We will not allow the reward of the reformers to be lost" (Al-Aʻrāf: 170).

Islam is Based on Submission

2- ودِنْ بكتابِ الله والسننِ التي ✱ أتت عنْ رسول الله تنجو وتربحُ

Devote yourself to Allah's book and the Sunan

conveyed by Allah's messenger to be safe and saved.

explanation

Submit as Allah has commanded "Enter into submission completely" (al-Baqara:208) and make your Dīn subject to the Quran and traditions of the Prophet Muhammad. The concept of having Dīn or being upon one's Dīn here means that your devotion, dedication, enthusiasm, and commitment to Islam is predicated on your submission to Allah's book and His messenger's Sunna. This will lead you to spiritual prosperity and success in both this life and the Hereafter.

Allah says: "So there will surely come to you guidance from Me, and whoever follows My guidance will neither go astray nor suffer" (Ṭāhā: 123).

Allah’s Speech is Uncreated

3- وقل غيرُ مخلوقٍ كلام مليكنا ❋ بذلك دان الأتقياء وأفصحوا

Say: Our Sovereign’s speech is not creation

The pious held this and it was their declaration

explanation

The Quran is Allah’s uncreated speech as revealed to Muḥammad. The claim that it was created, first proposed by the Jahmiyya, is an innovation. Other groups adapted this idea, attributing created speech to Allah like Ṣāliḥ’s camel is “Allah’s camel” (Hūd:64) or considering it a representation of divine speech. Ahl al-Sunnah refutes these views, affirming the Quran as uncreated.

Al-Imām Al-Lālakā’ī (418H), in "Sharḥ Usūl I‘tiqād Ahl al-Sunna wal Jamā‘a," lists over five hundred early scholars who declared that the Quran is uncreated and that anyone claiming otherwise is a disbeliever.

The author here tells the reader: When you speak about the Quran, you are to say it is uncreated as this is the faith position that the pious of the past took and it was the position they publicly proclaimed as well.

4- ولا تكُ في القرآن بالوقف قائلاً * كما قال أتْباعٌ لجهمٍ وأسجحُوا

About the Quran, do not take "pause" as a position, no.

like some followers of Jahm did, leaning thereto.

explanation

Don't take a position like the Wāqifa (a group of the Jahmiyya) that say "I'll abstain from saying whether the Quran is created or not" as a position, as an attempt to soften people to the idea that both beliefs are acceptable. By thinking that this issue is unimportant or not needing a decisive position, the unassailable nature of the Allah's speech and the veracity of revelation is endangered.

It is obligatory to clearly express the true belief indicated by the Quran and Sunnah. Failing to believe in it, or hesitating and wavering, is all deviation and misguidance. Allah says: "The believers are only those who have believed in Allah and His Messenger and then doubt not..." (Al-Ḥujurāt: 15). Hesitating to believe in the truth is a form of doubt and leads to disbelief.

Saying "My recitation of the Quran is created."

5- ولا تقل القرآن خلقٌ قرأْتُهُ ✱ فإن كلام اللهِ باللفظ يُوضحُ

Do not say "the Quran is a creation I recited"

For Allah's words by their enunciation are clarified.

explanation

Do not say "my recitation of the Quran is created," an innovation of the Lafẓiyya, a group of innovators who claimed their utterance of the Quran is created, to hide their innovated belief. Why? Because on one hand this person can mean the act of reciting (the movement of the tongue, etc.) and on the other he can mean what was recited (The Quran) is created. The former is acceptable, while the latter is false.

Ahl al-Sunnah says: The Quran is the speech of Allah, both its words and meanings. It is not merely the words without the meanings, nor the meanings without the words. The words are used to clarify the meanings, elucidate intentions, and manifest the intended message.

Allah Will Be Seen by the Believers

6- وقل يتجلى الله للخلقِ جهرةً ❋ كما البدر لا يخفى وربك أوضحُ

Declare that Allah to creation manifests appear,

Like the full moon's radiance, your Lord is more clear.

explanation

You should believe and state that Allah manifests to His creation on the Day of Judgment, and they will see him clearly, like one of you can see the full moon on a clear night. Allah blesses and honors the believers on the Day of Judgment with seeing Him. In fact, them seeing Him, exalted and high, is their highest aim and greatest goal.

In the Musnad of Aḥmad and the Sunan of al-Nasā'ī, it is narrated from Ammar ibn Yasir that the Prophet would supplicate, "O Allah, we ask You for the pleasure of gazing upon Your face and the longing to meet You without any harmful distress or misleading trial."

As for the disbelievers, they will not see Him, as indicated in His saying: "No! Indeed, from their Lord, that Day, they will be obscured." (Al-Muṭaffifīn: 15).

Negating Semblance in Allah's Attributes

7- وليس بمولدٍ وليس بوالدٍ ❋ وليس له شِبْهٌ تعالى المُسبحُ

Unbegotten, unbearing, He is beyond such scope,

No resemblance or offspring, to Allah is our highest hope.

explanation

Allah is the First and the Last, He does not beget nor is He begotten. He has no equal, no peer, and no comparable in His names, attributes, or actions.

Allah Almighty says: "There is nothing like unto Him, and He is the Hearing, the Seeing" (Ash-Shura: 11). He also says: "Do you know of any who is similar to Him?" (Maryam: 65). And He says: "And there is none comparable unto Him" (Al-Ikhlas: 4). And He says: "So do not attribute to Allah equals while you know" (Al-Baqarah: 22).

Affirming Allah's attributes does not necessitate likening Him to His creation.

Evidence is Found in Authentic Reports

8- وقد يُنكِر الجهمي هذا وعندنا ❋ بمصداقِ ما قلنا حديثٌ مصرحُ

Some Jahmis deny this, but we have in retort

what verifies the truth we say, an explicit report

explanation

The Jahmiyya also deny that Allah will be seen by His creation in the next life, an issue that is affirmed by explicit ḥadīth in which there is no difference about their authenticity.

From these hadith is the previously mentioned narration from Ammar ibn Yasir, as well as the coming hadith from Jarīr. The aḥādīth related to seeing Allah are Mutawātir; they were narrated by multiple companions of the Prophet (peace be upon him), including Abu Huraira, Abu Musa Al-Ash'arī, Jābir ibn 'Abdullah, and others.

Al-Shafi'ī said, "Whoever denies that Allah will be seen, is more deserving of being denied that blessing."

9- رواه جريرٌ عن مقالِ محمدٍ * فقُلْ مِثل ما قد قال في ذاك تنْجحُ -9

Narrated by Jarir from the words of Muhammad that precede

So say the same as he said, you will succeed.

explanation

The companion of the Prophet, Jarīr ibn ʻAbdullah al-Bajali, narrates that the Prophet said "Indeed, you will see your Lord as you see this full moon, and you will not be harmed by seeing Him. So, if you are able, do not miss performing the prayers before the sunrise and before the sunset." This is collected by al-Bukhāri and Muslim.

Comparing the attributes of the Creator to those of the creation, is known as the shirk of similarity. This contradicts the words of Allah: "So do not assert similarities to Allah. Indeed, Allah knows, and you do not know" (An-Nahl: 74). And He also says: "There is nothing like unto Him, and He is the Hearing, the Seeing" (Ash-Shura: 11).

Say what the companions said, not what innovators concocted later.

Allah’s Right Hand is Not Diminished

10- وقد ينكرُ الجهمي أيضاً يمينهُ ✱ وكِلتا يديه بالفواضلِ تنْفحُ

The Jahmiyya reject even His right as well,

Both his hands, filled with virtues, their bounties swell.

explanation

Muslim narrated in his Saḥīḥ that the Prophet (peace be upon him) said: "Indeed, the just ones will be upon pulpits of light, to the right of the Most Merciful, and both of His hands are right. Those who maintain justice in their rulings and their families and what they are responsible for." In another ḥadīth, “The right of Allah is bountiful not diminished, spending by day and night.” Allah says: "They have not appraised Allah with true appraisal, while the earth entirely will be within His grip on the Day of Resurrection, and the heavens will be folded in His right hand. Exalted is He and high above what they associate with Him" (Az-Zumar: 67).

The Jahmiyya deny these attributes, claiming that affirmation of what Allah Himself described Himself with compromises His transcendence and uniqueness.

This denial of the divine attributes stems from two things: 1) asserting similarities from the outset, 2) then making those assertions the basis for what they deem correct.

Allah’s Descends as Befits His Majesty

11- وقل ينزلُ الجبارُ في كلِّ ليلةٍ * بلا كيفَ جلَّ الواحدُ المتمَدحُ

Proclaim the Almighty descends every night,

With no “how” the One praised is alight.

explanation

Ahl al-Sunnah accepts Allah's attributes as stated in the Quran and Sunnah, affirming them as Allah and His Messenger did. Such affirmations do not require Allah to take on human form, nature, or attributes, as He transcends human limitations. While we understand descent and its meaning, here we do not describe it with any specific modality because it transcends our comprehension. Language provides a framework, and the true nature of divine actions remains beyond our understanding, as attribution necessitates particularization.

Recognizing our limited understanding of Allah's attributes does not render them meaningless, it acknowledges the limits of human understanding in capturing divine reality. We accept their truth as revealed, while their full essence remains beyond our comprehension.

The Evidence for This From Ḥadīth

12- إلى طبقِ الدنيا يمُنُّ بفضلِهِ ✱ فتفرجُ أبواب السماءِ وتُفتحُ

To the lowest heaven, He bestows His grace,

Unlocking celestial gates, unveiling space.

explanation

In the Musnad of Imam Aḥmad on the authority of Ibn Mas'ūd, Allah's Messenger said: "When a third of the night remains, Allah descends to the lowest heaven, then the gates of heaven are opened, then he spreads his hand and says: Is there a questioner who will be granted his request?... remaining like this until dawn rises."

Allah's Forgiveness & Bounty

13- يقولُ أَلا مُستغفرٌ يَلقَ غافراً * ومُستمنحٌ خيراً ورِزْقاً فيُمنحُ

Saying "Is there not seeker of pardon to find a Forgiver's grace,

And the one who seeks goodness, sustenance they embrace?"

explanation

Similar to the previous narration from the Musnad is another found in the Sunan of al-Tirmidhī: Allah says in the third part of the night "Is there any seeking forgiveness might that I forgive him? Is there anyone asking might that I give him? Is there anyone repenting might that I repent upon him?"

14- روى ذاك قومٌ لا يردُّ حديثُهم ❋ ألا خابَ قومٌ كذبوهم

Narrated by a group whose transmission cannot be rejected,

Alas, those who disbelieve them are condemned and dejected.

explanation

The fact that these narrations were transmitted to us by the companions of the Prophet and by the trustworthy and righteous scholars after them, casts aspersions on those that deny them. Where did they get their faith from if it wasn't from the companions?

'Abbād ibn al-Awām narrates: "Sharīk ibn 'Abdullah came to us about fifty years ago. I said to him: 'O Abu 'Abdullah, we have among us some people from the Mu'tazila who deny these hadiths.' He narrated to me about ten hadiths concerning this and said: 'As for us, we have taken our religion from the Tabi'īn, who took it from the Companions of the Messenger of Allah, so who did they take it from?'" This is authentically narrated in the Ibāna of Ibn Baṭṭa and Kitab al-Sunna of 'Abdullah ibn Aḥmad.

The Status of the Four Caliphs

15- وقل: إنَّ خيرَ النَّاسِ بعد محمَّدٍ * وزيراهُ قِدَماً ثم عثمانُ الارجَحُ

And say, "After Muhammad, the best of all,

his two ministers first, then Uthman's call

explanation

After Prophet Muhammad, the best of creation are his two ministers, those who were closest to him and staunchest in support of him, Abu Bakr al-Ṣiddīq and 'Umar ibn al-Khaṭṭāb, then comes 'Uthmān who is the 3rd most preferred when recalling the best of this Ummah.

Al-Bukhāri and Muslim narrated from the hadith of 'Amr ibn al-'Āṣ (may Allah be pleased with him) that he asked the Prophet (peace be upon him), "Who is the most beloved person to you?" He said, "'Āisha." I asked, "Among men?" He said, "Her father." I asked, "Then who?" He said, "'Umar ibn al-Khaṭṭāb."

In Saḥīḥ Al-Bukhāri from Ibn 'Umar (may Allah be pleased with him) that he said, "During the time of the Prophet (peace be upon him), we did not consider anyone equal to Abu Bakr, then 'Umar, then 'Uthmān, and then we left speaking of the companions of the Messenger of Allah (peace be upon him) without comparing them."

16- ورابعهُمْ خيرُ البريَّة بعدهُم * عليٌّ حليفُ الخيرِ بالخيرِ مُنْجِحُ

Fourth among them, the best of creations, he,

Ali, a paragon of good, in goodness' company.

explanation

The fourth of them in virtue is ‘Alī ibn Abī Ṭālib, the best of creation after these three, who was an ally of all things good, and succeeded in all good as well. The virtues of Ali ibn Abi Talib are too extensive to be denied and too numerous to be mentioned here.

Aḥmad narrates in his Musnad, as does al-Tirmidhī in his Sunan, from Zirr ibn Ḥubaysh that Ali said, “This is the Prophet’s covenant to me: No one loves him except for a believer, and no one hates him except a hypocrite.”

The Status of the Companions

17- وإنَّهم للرَّهطُ لا ريبَ فيهمُ * على نُجبِ الفردوسِ بالنُّور تَسرحُ

Indeed, they are the chosen ones, without doubt,

On the highest paradise, they bask, with light devout.

explanation

This group - Abu Bakr, 'Umar, 'Uthmān, and 'Ali - was chosen to follow the Prophet as his righteous successors and are no doubt in the highest part of paradise just as they held the highest level of esteem in this life, as they were promised paradise by the Prophet himself.

Anyone who doubts their entrance into Paradise and their favored position with Allah has doubted the Messenger of Allah himself.

18- سعيدٌ وسعدٌ وابن عوفٍ وطلحةٌ * وعامرُ فهرٍ والزبيرُ الممدَّح

Sa'id, Sa'd, Ibn 'Awf, and Talha, the honored,

'Āmir of Fihr, Zubayr, their virtues are uncovered.

explanation

After the first four are six more of the companions, making up the ten promised paradise as found in the ḥadīth of Abu Sa'īd in al-Tirmidhī, "Abu Bakr is in Paradise, and 'Umar is in Paradise, and 'Uthmān is in Paradise, and 'Alī is in Paradise, and Ṭalḥa is in Paradise, and Al-Zubayr is in Paradise, and 'AbdulRaḥmān ibn 'Awf is in Paradise, and Sa'd is in Paradise, and Sa'īd is in Paradise, and Abu Ubayda ibn al-Jarrāḥ is in Paradise."

'Āmir of Fihr is Abu 'Ubayda.

Revering and Respecting the Companions

19- وقل خير قولٍ في الصحابة كلِّهم ❋ ولا تك طعَّاناً تعيبُ وتجرحُ

Proclaim the best speech about the companions as a whole,

Refrain from slander and harm, let respect be your goal.

explanation

When speaking about the Companions of the Prophet, it is essential for those adhering to the Sunnah to maintain a respectful stance. They should not harbor any ill feelings in their hearts towards them.

A believer's speech about them should be kind and their language should remain pure, avoiding criticism and refraining from delving into the disputes that may have arisen among the Companions. Instead, they should choose words that foster a deeper affection for the Companions in their hearts and the hearts of others.

The Evidence for the Companions' Status

20- فقد نطقَ الوحيُ المبين بفضلِهم ✱ وفي الفتح آيٌ للصَّحابةِ تمدحُ

Of their nobility the clear revelation does imbue,

And In victory's surah, verses extol their virtue.

explanation

Revelation is replete with evidence highlighting the virtues of the Companions. The author points to verses in Surah Al-Fath that praise the Companions and elucidate their merits. One such verse is the beginning of the Surah: "It is He who sent down tranquility into the hearts of the believers, that they would increase in faith along with their faith...." (al-Fatḥ:4) Then later He states "Indeed, those who pledge allegiance to you, they are actually pledging allegiance to Allah. The hand of Allah is over their hands." (al-Fatḥ:10) He then says, "Indeed God is pleased with the believers as they pledged allegiance to you under the tree, knowing what was in their hearts he sent down tranquility upon them and recompensed them with a close victory." (al-Fatḥ:18).

If Allah was and is pleased with them, why would anyone not be?

Belief in Qadr, a Pillar of Faith

21- وبالقدرِ المقدورِ أيقِن فإنَّه ✱ دعامةُ عقدِ الدِّين والدِّينُ أفيحُ

Of the preordained decree, be certain and affirm,

It's a pillar of faith, on which our religion is firm.

explanation

This stanza affirms the sixth pillar of faith, which is belief in predestination (Qadar), as stated in the well-known Ḥadīth of Jibrīl: "Faith is to believe in Allah, His angels, His books, His messengers, the Last Day, and Qadr, its good and bad." Ibn Abbas stated, "Qadr is the structure of monotheism. Whoever believes in Allah's Oneness and denies Qadr has breached his Tawḥīd."

In other words, without belief in Qadr, true monotheism is incomplete. Rejecting Qadr is tantamount to rejecting Allah, as Imam Aḥmad has said. The innovation of rejecting Qadr was the second innovation to arise in the Umma after the innovation of the Khawārij.

Belief in the Last Day and All It Entails

22- ولا تُنكِرَنْ جهلاً نكيراً ومُنكراً * ولا الحوْضَ والميزانَ إنّك تُنصحُ

Deny not the angels Munkar and Nakīr ignorantly

Nor the Pond and the Scale, you've been advised eloquently.

explanation

Belief in the Last Day, i.e. Belief in everything that Allah and His Messenger informed us of regarding what will occur after death, is one of the six pillars of faith. It starts from the moment of death and belief that the angels Munkar and Nakīr will come to the deceased to question him, to the plains of the Day of Judgment where the Pond (al-Ḥawḍ) and the Fount (al-Kawthar) granted to the Prophet will be, to the Scales (al-Mīzān) that will weigh creation's deeds, to entrance to Heaven or Hell.

The Sunnī affirms all these issues as they are found in the Sunna of the Prophet, and the Bid'ī explains them away or denies them.

Allah's Favor on the People of Tawḥīd

23- وقُلْ يُخرِجُ اللهُ الْعظيمُ بِفَضلِهِ * مِنَ النارِ أجْساداً مِنَ الفَحْمِ تُطرحُ

Say, By His grace, Allah Almighty will retrieve,

From the fire, bodies as coal, He shall relieve.

explanation

Those who commit major sins will eventually be taken from the hellfire by Allah's grace, their bodies having burnt to a crisp and turned to charcoal. Allah will take them from the hellfire, although they have no redeeming good deeds, and they will be admitted to Paradise.

This is taken from the long ḥadīth of Abu Sa'īd in Saḥīḥ al-Bukhāri, which outlines the sequence of events on the Day of Judgment.

Those Who Enter Paradise Despite No Actions

24- عَلى النهرِ في الفِرْدوسِ تَحْيَا بِمَائِهِ * كَحِبِّ حَمِيلِ السَّيْلِ إِذْ جَاءَ يَطْفَحُ

On the riverbanks of paradise, they will enliven and grow

Like a seed strewn from a flood when waters flow

explanation

The ḥadīth of Abu Sa'īd mentions that after the People of Paradise enter Paradise and the People of Hell enter Hell, Allah will remove from the hellfire those with a mustard's seed of faith in their hearts; their charcoaled bodies will be strewn into the "River of Life" in Paradise. They will regenerate like a seed strewn onto the shore after a flood regenerates, part of it being discolored until it is whole and sprouts life. The people of Paradise will say "These are those emancipated by al-Raḥmān, He entered them into Paradise with no actions they performed or good they put forward." This is narrated by al-Bukhāri and Muslim.

Prophet’s Intercession / Punishment of the Grave

25- وإن رسولَ اللهِ للخَلْقِ شَافِعٌ * وقُلْ في عَذابِ القَبْرِ حَقّ موُضحُ

The Messenger intercedes for all creation's plight,

Proclaim the reality of the grave's torment, truth alight.

explanation

After death and the questioning of the grave, those that are deserving of it will be punished in their graves, as Allah refers to Pharoah and his people in Surat Ghāfir verse 46. In al-Bukhāri from the hadith of ‘Āisha, “Yes, the punishment of the grave is true.” Then on the Day of Judgment, the Messenger will be an intercessor for all of creation, imploring Allah to begin the judgment and end the torment of that day. He will also intercede specifically for the believers on that day, saying “My Ummah, Oh Lord!” and Allah will command him to enter his Ummah, those that have no accounting upon them, into Paradise.

Not Excommunicating Believers Due to Sin

26- وَلَا تُكَفِّرَنْ أَهْلَ الصَّلاةِ وإِنْ عَصَوْا ✱ فَكُلُّهُمُ يَعْصِي وذُو العَرْشِ يَصْفَحُ

Do not deem prayerful people as disbelieving souls,

For everyone errs, yet the Throne's Master consoles.

explanation

Sinful people of the Ummah are not disbelievers for their sins, as long as they pray and avoid Shirk. All humans are sinful, and the best of the sinful are those that repent. Allah, the One, the Dominant, the Master of the exalted throne, above His creation, is Clement, forgives, and accepts the repentance of those that repent; only He has the ability to forgive them.

Takfīr, the act of pronouncing an individual to be outside of the fold of Islam, is a Shar'ī ruling. Such pronouncements should only be made based on evidence and by qualified people, not based on whims or suppositions.

The differences about the status of sinners were one of the first issues that arose in Islamic history.

The Misguidance of the Khawārij

27- وَلَا تَعتقِدْ رأيَ الخَوَارجِ إنهُ ✱ مقَالٌ لِمَنْ يَهواهُ يُردي ويَفْضَحُ

Do not heed the Khawārij's misguided disgrace,

Words that destroy those that admire their base.

explanation

Beware of the Khawārij, those that renegaded against ʻAlī ibn Abī Talib, differed with the Sunna, claimed to have knowledge of the Quran greater than those it was revealed among, excommunicated those that commit major sins, and claimed that people who commit major sins are disbelievers who will be eternally damned to the hellfire on the Day of Judgment.

Anyone who follows the path and ideology of the Khawarij is not worthy of admiration or respect.

The Misguidance of the Murjia

28- ولا تكُ مُرْجيًّا لَعُوبا بدينهِ ❋ ألاَ إِنمَا المُرْجِي بِالدينِ يَمْزحُ

Do not be a Murji' who mocks his faith's creed,

Indeed, he is one whose jest shall mislead.

explanation

The Murji'a, those that claim that actions are not part of faith, are merely kidding themselves. They claim that committing sins does not harm one's faith, just as obedience does not benefit one with disbelief. According to them, faith is merely knowledge.

There is no greater jest and mockery of faith than a person who claims faith while opening the door to sins and destructive actions that fly in the face of faith, claiming that nothing they do, whether mundane or sinful, influences their faith.

Faith is Comprised of Beliefs and Actions

29- وقلْ : إنمَا الإِيمانُ : قولٌ ونيةٌ ✱ وفعلٌ عَلَى قولِ النبي مُصَرحُ

Say, "Indeed, faith is in words, intentions too,

Actions aligned with the Prophet's teachings, true."

explanation

The creed of Ahl al-Sunnah regarding faith is that it is based on three pillars: belief in the heart, declaration with the tongue, and actions of both the heart and limbs. A multitude of evidence from the Quran and the Sunnah indicates the inclusion of these three elements in faith.

From this evidence is the narration of Abu Hurayra, "Imān has seventy-odd branches, the uppermost of which is the declaration: La ilaha illallah, and the least of which is removing harmful things from the road. And shyness is a branch of faith."

Faith Increases and Decreases

30- وَيَنْقُصُ طوراً بالمَعَاصِي وتَارةً ❋ بِطَاعَتِهِ يَنْمِي وفي الوَزْنِ يَرْجَحُ

Sometimes diminished by sins, it wanes,

Through obedience, it increases, the balance maintains.

explanation

Faith is at times decreased by sins, but when one is obedient it increases. From the narrations about this is that reported from ‘Umayr ibn Ḥabīb al-Khaṭmi that he said, "Faith increases and decreases." He was asked, "What is its increase and decrease?" He said, "When we mention Allah, praise Him, and glorify Him, that is its increase. And when we are heedless and forget, that is its decrease." Ibn Abī Shayba narrated this in Kitab al-Īmān.

Through good deeds our scales are heavy on the day of judgment, and through sins they are light.

Avoiding Personal Opinion in Faith

31- ودعْ عَنْكَ آراءَ الرجالِ وقَوْلَهُمْ * فقولُ رسولِ اللهِ أزكَى وأَشْرحُ

Disregard human opinions, their words and views,

For the Prophet's sayings are purer, clarity ensues.

explanation

Do not build your faith and beliefs on the concocted opinions of men, instead build them on the Book and the Sunnah as doing so embodies knowledge, safety, and more decisive.

As ‘Umar ibn al-Khaṭṭāb said "Beware of people of opinion, as they are enemies of the faith; they were unable to preserve the Sunnah and so they took to their personal views." This is narrated by Abu Dāwūd.

Embodying High Character and Avoiding Flippancy

32- ولا تَكُ مِن قوْمٍ تلهوْا بدينِهِمْ * فَتَطْعَنَ في أهلِ الحَديثِ وتقدحُ

Do not be among those who trivialize their faith,

Avoid criticizing the people of Ḥadīth, no disdain beneath.

explanation

From the character of Ahl al-Sunna is that they do not take their faith lightly, treating it flippantly. Those who trivialize their faith include innovators who concoct for themselves a faith that wasn't sanctioned by Allah and His messenger, as well as the immoral who do not hold their Lord, His messenger, and their faith in esteem. They mock and accuse the People of Ḥadīth of ignorance, and they insult people inclined to good and nobility. The lesson here is to do the opposite of all this.

The person who venerates the Sunnah holds the highest character, follows the Prophet's example, and seeks to always embody the best of character. He seeks to emulate the Prophet when Allah said about him, "Indeed you are upon lofty character." (al-Qalam:4)

Taking This Creed to Heart

33- إِذَا مَا اعْتَقَدْتَ الدهْرَ يا صَاحِ هذِهِ ❋ فَأَنْت عَلَى خَيْرٍ تبيتُ وتُصْبِحُ

When you – oh friend – hold on and believe this way,

You shall rest easy and wake to a brighter day.

explanation

If you can adhere to this creed taken from the Quran and the Sunnah of the Messenger and follow in the footsteps of the Pious that followed him, then you will be following good and will be on the correct faith, day in and day out.

The person who believes in Allah, follows His messenger, leaves off his desires, and does righteous deeds will reap the rewards; in this life he will have a restful heart and an enlivened life, and in the next he will be rewarded with Paradise and the company of the Prophet.

Ibn Abī Dāwūd's proclamation of his creed

Abu Bakr Ibn Abī Dāwūd then said to us:

ثم قال لنا أبو بكر بن أبي داود :

هذا قولي وقول أبي وقول أحمد بن حنبل وقول من أدركنا من أهل العلم

ومن لم ندرك ممن بلغنا عنه ، فمن قال عليّ غير هذا فقد كذب .

This is my belief, and the belief of my father, and the belief of Aḥmad ibn Ḥanbal, and the belief of the scholars we've met, and that of the scholars we have not met but was transmitted to us from them; anyone claiming about me other than this has lied.

انتهى كلامه رحمه الله

Translator's Note

قال مترجمها أبو لقمان: وهو ما أدين الله به من اعتقاد وأسأله أن يميتني عليه، فبه توفيقي وإليه أمري، وقد فرغت من ترجمته والتعليق عليه ليلة الجمعة السادس عشر من شهر صفر الخير، سنة ألف وأربعمائة وخمس وأربعين من هجرة المصطفى.

Abu Luqmaan, its translator, said: This is what I take as my faith and ask Allah that I die upon these beliefs. With Him is my success, and to Him I entrust my affairs. I completed its translation and explanation on the night of Friday, the sixteenth of Ṣafar Al-Khayr in the year one thousand four hundred and forty of the Hijra of the Chosen Prophet, peace and blessings be upon him, and upon his family and companions, in abundance.

وصلّى الله على

نَبيّنا محمدٍ المُجْتبى

وعلى آله وصَحْبِهِ

وسلّم تسليمًا

كثيرًا.

www.ingramcontent.com/pod-product-compliance
Lightning Source LLC
Chambersburg PA
CBHW072055040426
42447CB00012BB/3128
* 9 7 9 8 9 8 9 8 6 9 6 2 6 *